Library Technology
REPORTS
Expert Guides to Library Systems and Services

Digital Media and Library Instruction

Edited by Heather Moorefield-Lang

ALA TechSource
alatechsource.org

American Library Association

Library Technology
REPORTS

ALA TechSource purchases fund advocacy, awareness, and accreditation programs for library professionals worldwide.

Volume 55, Number 5
Digital Media and Library Instruction
ISBN: 978-0-8389-1818-0

American Library Association
50 East Huron St.
Chicago, IL 60611-2795 USA
alatechsource.org
800-545-2433, ext. 4299
312-944-6780
312-280-5275 (fax)

Advertising Representative
Samantha Imburgia
simburgia@ala.org
312-280-3244

Editor
Samantha Imburgia
simburgia@ala.org
312-280-3244

Copy Editor
Judith Lauber

Production
ALA Production Services

Cover Design
Alejandra Diaz and ALA Production Services

Library Technology Reports (ISSN 0024-2586) is published eight times a year (January, March, April, June, July, September, October, and December) by American Library Association, 50 E. Huron St., Chicago, IL 60611. It is managed by ALA TechSource, a unit of the publishing department of ALA. Periodical postage paid at Chicago, Illinois, and at additional mailing offices. POSTMASTER: Send address changes to Library Technology Reports, 50 E. Huron St., Chicago, IL 60611.

ALA TechSource
alatechsource.org

About the Editor

Heather Moorefield-Lang is an assistant professor with the Department of Library and Information Studies in the School of Education at the University of North Carolina at Greensboro. She has long been interested in how technologies can enhance instruction in libraries and classroom, both face-to-face and online. To learn more about Moorefield-Lang and her work, see her website https://www.techfifteen.com, check out her YouTube channel *Tech 15*, or follow her on Twitter @actinginthelib.

Abstract

Professionals in the field of librarianship are creative when it comes to the delivery of information and instruction. If face-to-face options aren't available, we take to digital means, and there are so many options out there. Podcasting, vlogging, and edutubing are just some of them. In this issue of *Library Technology Reports* (vol. 55, no. 5), read about a librarian and his podcast, a blogging librarian, a library professor with educational YouTube channels, and recommendations for strong flipped instruction delivery from the classroom or library.

Subscriptions

alatechsource.org/subscribe

Contents

Contents, continued

Chapter 1

Introduction

Heather Moorefield-Lang

"We need to bring learning to people instead of people to learning."

—*Elliott Masie, MASIE Center*

Library instruction arrives in a variety of forms. It can be face-to-face instruction of information literacy skills to middle school students in a K–12 library. Classes can be taught by librarian liaisons at a university as they train students in research skills, citations, evaluation of sources, and so much more. Library instruction can be found in professional development. Through peer training, we teach each other a variety of skills and share information across the amazing professional learning network of librarians, paraprofessionals, library directors, and professors.

In our field, it is vital to stay current and up-to-date, especially when it comes to teaching and technology. To be current means seeking out the continuously changing trends and programs while also maintaining a balance of traditions.[1] Finding opportunities to delve into professional development and new information is always a challenge. Is the training on campus or online? Can it be found at a local university or college, or in the city of current residence? Is there a cost to the professional development or information sought? No matter the challenge, we continue to seek training so we can be better instructors, librarians, and educators.

With technology venues like blogging, podcasting, online course management systems, and unified communication services like Zoom, delivery methods for information and professional development continue to grow and change. Podcasts are digital audio files that can be found and downloaded on the internet.[2] Zoom and other unified communication services offer users the opportunity to post or view video, chat, and share information with individuals or groups. These items can be documented, shared, and linked for future viewing or reading, and they offer a multitude of opportunities in the delivery of information, instruction, and professional development across the field of librarianship regardless of location, language, or ability.

Information

How do we deliver information and instruction in libraries and library instruction? It is important to think about how we deliver information to our learners. Are we teaching a face-to-face class? Is the instruction being distributed through a digital medium? Are we teaching in real time (synchronous) or not (asynchronous)? Research and theory on the dissemination of information dates to the 1920s.[3] Researchers specifically were looking at the distribution of information. When we look at the delivery of information, whether it be for instruction, professional development, or mastery of skill, we need to think about these four factors: the audience or user, the source of the delivery, the content of the information, and the type of media or technology being used to deliver the information.[4] In other words, when deciding how to share information in our field, first we must consider whom we are addressing. Information given to second graders would be offered very differently from information for a group of our peers or a room full of library directors. We must think about where our information is coming from and, as professionals in the field of librarianship, ensure that our information is fully vetted and correct, which leads to the content of our information—what we wish to share and how much. We also want to make sure that we offer enough information or instruction without overloading our learners. We complete our sharing by choosing the type of media or technology to best deliver the information. As you will see in this issue of *Library Technology Reports,* the authors showcase a wide range of technologies to disseminate information and instruction to their students, peers, and patrons.

Content

In this report, we look at digital media and library instruction. *Digital media* is a term that runs the gamut of technology and content when it comes to instruction and information. For this technology report, we look specifically at instruction and information being delivered in library settings or by librarians and their peer educators. Steve Thomas discusses his podcast *Circulating Ideas* and introduces us to the idea of podcasting in the field of librarianship. He takes us through the process of podcasting and what is needed to put together your own production. Lucy Green delves into research and information on flipped instruction. She introduces the concept, discusses how it can be used in teaching, and shares best practices. Later in this report, I discuss my YouTube channels *Tech Fifteen* and *Research Xpress* and address education-based YouTubing (edutubing), how to create your own channel, and good practices. Lucas Maxwell finishes this report with his background in blogging. He discusses his inspiration to start a blog, tips for getting started, and ideas for involving students in the blogging process.

There is something for everyone in this report. Authors are from K–12 settings, public libraries, and schools of library science. Regardless of their background, the focus remains the same—digital media and instruction for the field of librarianship.

Audience

I envision the readers of this issue of *Library Technology Reports* to be librarians, educators, preservice librarians, and professors of library science. This report is for anyone looking to find ideas and concepts in the area of technology, media, and instruction, be it in a library or a classroom. Though the authors of this technology report are mainly from the field of library science, our information can easily cross disciplines. Every chapter was written with an audience in mind because each author worked with a certain population, but the ideas are applicable to a wider group of recipients. This report was written to generate and share ideas as well as inspire our readers to think about how to make instruction and information available to peer librarians, educators, students, and library patrons, as well as faculty and staff.

Notes

1. Lisa Shamchuk, "Professional Development on a Budget: Facilitating Learning Opportunities for Information Literacy Instruction," *Partnership: The Canadian Journal of Librarian and Information Practice and Research* 10, no. 1 (2015): 1–14.
2. Steve Thomas, "Hearing Voices: Librarian-Produced Podcasts," *American Libraries Magazine*, January 4, 2016, http://americanlibrariesmagazine.org/2016/01/04/hearing-voices-librarian-produced-podcasts.
3. National Center for the Dissemination of Disability Research, *Developing an Effective Dissemination Plan* (Austin, TX: National Center for the Dissemination of Disability Research, Southwest Educational Development Laboratory, 2003), 4, cited in Barb Garner, Marco Boscolo, John Comings, Donna Curry, Kelly McClure, and Cristine Smith, *An Evaluation of the NCSALL Publication* Focus on Basics, NCSALL Reports #27 (Cambridge, MA: National Center for the Study of Adult Learning and Literacy [NCSALL], Harvard Graduate School of Education, January 2006), 5, http://eric.ed.gov/?id=ED491152.
4. National Center for the Dissemination of Disability Research, *Developing an Effective Dissemination Plan*, cited in Garner et al., *An Evaluation of the NCSALL Publication* Focus on Basics, 5.

Chapter 2

Library-Podcast Intersections

Steve Thomas*

A library, at its core, is not just a collection of ideas but also an institution that provides the means to develop and contextualize new knowledge. Similarly, a podcast is not just an audio file distributed over the internet but also a tool that creates conversations, generating new ideas and concepts.

The links between libraries and podcasts are more prevalent than might be apparent at first blush. Libraries fill the world with stories, whether in the striking text of a physical volume or through the mellifluous words of a children's librarian during storytime. Many of the most popular podcasts have scaled their way to the top of the charts by telling an engaging true crime story or humorously poking holes in our culture through drunken retellings of the past. Just as most libraries carry popular materials, a podcast can also entertain as its main goal.

Libraries and podcasts also have the potential to be remarkable facilitators of learning. Both thrive on satiating curiosities and exploring one's own imagination through reading, attending a program, or creating in a makerspace, filling the voids that users may not even be aware they have. Libraries have historically been engines of education, and podcasts, though a much newer phenomenon than libraries, also generate learning opportunities for their listeners, whether navigating listeners through a fraught election season, guiding nascent runners on their fitness journey, or digging deep into how stuff works.

Intersections

Until recently, intersections between libraries and podcasts have been infrequent. A few universities used podcasts to dole out homework assignments a decade back but quickly abandoned this method of distribution. In 2005, South Huntington Public Library in Long Island, New York, allowed its patrons to check out iPods with audiobooks preloaded on them.[1] Most of the early library podcasts were produced by individual librarians on their own time, not as part of their regular job at an institution. However, there are exceptions, such as Maurice Coleman's *T Is for Training*, which is the longest-running library podcast and provides a place for librarians to bring up training issues, among other professional concerns, in a supportive roundtable discussion.[2]

Library podcasts generally fall into two categories: patron-focused or professional development. This chapter will deal mainly in the latter category due to my work on the *Circulating Ideas* podcast. However, focusing on patrons is an equally valid and exciting form of podcasting. Many of these podcasts are officially produced and distributed from their institutions, such as the Library of Congress, publishers, and even vendors like OverDrive.

The most popular podcasts produced by librarians as part of their work for patrons are edited versions of live events such as on-stage interviews with authors, for example, at the National Book Festival from the Library of Congress. Other public libraries that preserve the talks done by outside speakers as podcasts include Los Angeles (CA) Public Library's *ALOUD* at the Central Library, the *Free Library Podcast* from the Free Library of Philadelphia (PA), and the *NYPL Podcast*.[3]

Others will broadcast about upcoming library and community events or feature various library staff members talking about their work. Universal College of Learning's library in Palmerston North, New Zealand, did an experiment with podcasting in 2006 to provide instructional materials to its patrons, such as orientation tours and information on how to use the online catalog. A teacher outside Washington, DC, shared her excitement about podcasting with her students, leading the students to create their own podcast

* **Steve Thomas** is a branch manager at Gwinnett County (GA) Public Library. Since 2011, he has produced the *Circulating Ideas* podcast, where he facilitates conversions about how libraries remain relevant and vibrant in the twenty-first century. You can find out more about his podcast by visiting https://circulatingideas.com and by following *Circulating Ideas* on Twitter @circideas.

called *100% Kids*, talking about fairness and injustice. The Escondido Public Library collects and shares local knowledge in its *LibraryYOU* podcast. Recently, I started a podcast called *Flip the Library* at my place of work, where a colleague and I focus on the work our staff does; it is intended mostly for our internal staff but is publicly available for our community as well.

Another popular genre of patron-centered library podcasts revolves around readers' advisory. One innovative example is Arlington (VA) Public Library's *Big Book Club* podcast, a virtual book club that first made its way through *War and Peace* 100 pages at a time and then tackled *Middlemarch*, complete with live Facebook discussions between library staff and their community, along with an accompanying podcast with library staff giving their impressions of the text. OverDrive's *Professional Book Nerds* offers personal recommendations from OverDrive staff, and HarperCollins releases the *Library Love Fest* podcast, which focuses exclusively on titles in its catalog but often offers an inside look at the process by having editors interview the authors with whom they work.

Independent librarians also produce some of the best readers' advisory podcasts. Renata Sancken and Kait Sudol host the *Worst Bestsellers* podcast, where they read popular books of questionable quality, or, as their tagline states, "We read stuff so you don't have to." Matthew Winner's *Children's Book Podcast* is, as expected, about children's books and features interviews with the authors who write them. The *Book Club for Masochists* chooses a genre at random monthly and reads a few titles in that genre to discuss in a group setting, which sometimes leads to pleasant surprises, and sometimes not.

The previously mentioned *T Is for Training* is done as part of Coleman's work as technical trainer at Harford County (MD) Public Library, but most other library podcasts that pursue professional development goals are more likely produced by independent librarians. The now-defunct *Adventures in Library Instruction* featured academic librarians focused on bibliographic instructional issues. *Beyond the Stacks*, which was funded through an IMLS grant, focused on the variety of careers available to library and information professionals. Daniel Messer's *Cyberpunk Librarian* talks about using high-tech, low-budget ideas for your library. *The Library Pros* podcast puts the focus on library professionals and the work that they do. Library professional organizations have also gotten into the act in recent years, with the American Library Association's *Dewey Decibel* podcast and the Public Library Association's *FYI* podcast.

Since 2011, I have produced the *Circulating Ideas* podcast, which facilitates conversations about the innovative people and ideas allowing libraries to thrive in the twenty-first century. Most guests work in libraries and discuss their experience, but others with a link to libraries have also been featured, such as author Cory Doctorow, thought leader David Weinberger, and journalists Clive Thompson, Andy Ihnatko, and David Beard. The focus is on lighting a beacon to reveal the many paths toward the future of libraries by interviewing the people doing the work.

Process

To understand the process of creating and distributing a podcast, it is necessary to have a basic understanding of the technical infrastructure underlying the podcasting ecosystem. Though video podcasts ("vodcasts") exist, for the most part, podcasts are spoken-word audio files, like talk radio on the internet. They are primarily in the open standard MP3 format, which allows the audio to be compressed to a small size with acceptable fidelity to the source material, which saves bandwidth costs to users who either download or stream the files.[4]

Podcasts are distributed via RSS, which stands for either "Rich Site Summary" or "Really Simple Syndication," depending on who you ask. RSS creates a feed that allows the user to subscribe to a source of information on the internet and receive new content as it is posted to that source. A podcast app, sometimes called a podcatcher, will take that RSS feed and either automatically download or provide the user a notification when new content, such as a new episode of a podcast, is posted on the source. Most podcast listeners consume podcasts via smartphone apps, such as Apple Podcasts, Stitcher, Spotify, or Overcast, among others, but podcast episodes can often be streamed from a website in a browser as well.

But what about the initial creation of the podcast?

Libraries and podcasts share another key aspect: they can be, and often by necessity are, shoestring operations. It's actually an advantage of podcasting that it can be done in a low-cost way, as it allows a lower barrier to access.[5] I have been fortunate enough to have supportive listeners and some generous sponsors to partially fund the production of my show, allowing me to upgrade equipment and software to provide better audio and more convenient recording options, but with a few foundational technologies, anyone can get started with podcasting, and it gets easier and more convenient every day.

The one required piece of technology is a microphone to record the audio for the podcast, though for the budget-conscious, that microphone may be the one inside their phone or computer. An external microphone, either in a handheld recorder like a Zoom h4n or one that plugs in via USB or XLR cables, will drastically improve the sound quality, as will the use of a pop filter, which offers protection for the microphone from fast-moving air like wind or aspirated human speech. The type of microphone purchased depends on the use case.

Many podcasts with more than one host or with guests are recorded over the internet via Skype or Google Hangouts, while others are recorded face-to-face. Audio can also be captured via traditional phone calls.

Quickly, producers of burgeoning podcasts will learn that they would do well to add or upgrade other hardware and software. Editing software allows the producer to improve sound quality and add in additional music tracks or other audio. Many free options are available, with one of the most popular being Audacity, an open-source solution that works on all major desktop operating systems, including Linux. Apple's GarageBand comes bundled free with all Macintosh computers running macOS; an iOS version with fewer features is also a free option for users of Apple mobile devices.

For the *Circulating Ideas* podcast, I have a Blue Yeti microphone that plugs into my iMac via USB-A and has a pop filter, and I edit the audio using Apple's professional editing software Logic. I use the Forecast app to convert my file to MP3 and to add chapters and episode-specific art. Most episodes are recorded over Skype with eCamm's Call Recorder app; when recording a phone call, I use Audio Hijack from Rogue Amoeba. For the best audio, I will sometimes ask my guests to record their end of the conversation on their computer and send me the file, and then I combine that with my track to recreate the conversation. In person, I record either on my iPad with the Ferrite Recording Studio or Twisted Wave app, or with a handheld digital recorder called a Zoom h4n, which records onto a standard SD card that is easily transferable to my iMac.

Audience

If a podcast is recorded and no one listens, does it make a sound?

The next step to gaining an audience for your podcast, even if it is restricted, is to find it a home on the internet. Producers who run their own servers may choose to upload their file there, or they may pick from a wide array of hosting platforms, many of which cater directly to the podcast market. These specialized hosts facilitate the generation of RSS feeds and provide valuable statistics, such as how many downloads episodes get and the geographic location of those downloads; these statistics may be a valuable asset if a library is asked for quantifiable data to justify its podcasting efforts.

My host of choice is the Internet Archive, which has the benefits of being free and robust enough to feel secure in its long-term vitality. Other popular hosting options are Libsyn, Podbean, and SoundCloud. Since the Internet Archive does not generate an RSS feed for my content, I turn to Google's FeedBurner, which picks up new posts on my WordPress site and pushes them to the feed for consumers to download on their devices, in their apps of choice.

Podcasts, for all their positives, also have some drawbacks that must be addressed, the main one being accessibility.[6] For many of those with hearing impairments, a podcast is not going to be an option, though many podcasts, including my own, offer text transcripts to open up the content of the shows to those with hearing impairments or those who do not learn well from audio. Transcripts on the web also increase discoverability because search engines cannot crawl an audio file (yet!) and rely on text to properly index pages. Blind and low-vision patrons may also encounter roadblocks, but podcasters can help alleviate them by following accessibility standards; also, smart speakers with voice assistants like Amazon's Echo devices or Apple's HomePod can be another solution for these patrons.

Another accessibility hurdle—that podcasts require an internet connection—can be a barrier to those across the digital divide who do not have internet-enabled devices or lack the knowledge of how to find and listen to podcasts. Libraries assist with this by offering patrons free Wi-Fi access.

Content

A podcast needs a purpose, or no one will want to listen. For librarians, there are many options, as mentioned earlier, but they all share the idea of sharing knowledge and learning, and podcasting can be an invaluable formal or informal instructional tool. Formally, podcasts can distribute homework assignments or guide the learner through a difficult piece of work, providing audio annotations to a text or work of art. They can function in the role of course reserves and offer a wider range of options, such as playing music clips or important speeches. Podcasts could also be used to assist patrons in using library resources or finding out about upcoming events or programs of interest. Informally, podcasts can be used more as I do, to facilitate casual, professional conversations about a wide range of topics, or provide water cooler discussion fodder.

I started my podcast because I was inspired by the work of other librarians and wanted as many people as possible to know about that work, to break the stereotypes of the profession and let the world know about the real work being done in libraries in the modern age. In my wildest dreams, the show would reach beyond libraryland and would change civilian attitudes about how libraries had changed since their childhood. As it is, the show's audience is primarily people working in libraries, but that provides the profession with that same inspiration that drove me to start the show in the first place. Having role models can be a powerful motivator and can generate creative new ideas in your own work.

In the course of my regular professional reading, I keep notes on names of librarians whose writing appeals to me. This reading includes not only publications such as *Library Journal*, *American Libraries*, and *Publishers Weekly*, but also social media; I am a member of a small number of library groups on Facebook, and most of my Twitter follows are of other librarians or others who might influence the profession. *Library Journal*'s annual Movers and Shakers list is a prime source for adding new voices to my potential guest list. I also peruse the catalogs of ALA Publishing, ABC-CLIO's Libraries Unlimited, and other library-centric publishers for trends that they are covering with books and reports.

I take a conversational tone with guests to make them feel more comfortable and to make listening a more pleasant, entertaining experience. The librarians and library-adjacent guests on my podcast inform the listeners about topics ranging from setting up a makerspace to planning an engaging story time for children with developmental disabilities, from driving civilians to the polls to support their local library to fighting fake news. When planning a podcast, remember your audience. Think about who you are speaking to, the tone you might like to use, and ways to draw in an audience.

Conclusion

In one final key way, libraries and podcasts intersect by fostering community. The patrons of a library and the listeners of a podcast come together to share their love of learning and the joys of discovery. Just as a library does outreach to its community, including through its curated collections, there is a connection between podcast producers and their audience and interweaving connections among the audience itself. Often, these communities don't meet in the same physical space, as is the wont of the twenty-first-century citizen, but come together in an intellectual sense to share in a collective knowledge, and occasionally meet in the physical world at library programs or live podcast recordings.

As librarians are scattered throughout the country and around the world, podcasts can bring them together to learn and grow in common.

Circulating Ideas Resources: The Tech That Makes This Particular Podcast Happen

- *Circulating Ideas*, https://circulatingideas.com
- Blue: Yeti Microphones, https://www.bluedesigns.com
- Logic Pro X, https://www.apple.com/logic-pro
- Forecast, https://overcast.fm/forecast
- Ecamm Call Recorder, https://www.ecamm.com/mac/callrecorder
- Audio Hijack, https://rogueamoeba.com/audiohijack
- Ferrite Recording Studio, https://www.wooji-juice.com/products/ferrite
- TwistedWave, https://twistedwave.com
- Zoom H4n, https://www.zoom.co.jp/products/handy-recorder/h4nsp-handy-recorder

Recommended Library-Themed Podcasts

- *T Is for Training*, https://tisfortraining.wordpress.com
- Library of Congress Podcasts, https://www.loc.gov/podcasts
- *Big Book Club*, http://bigbookclub.libsyn.com
- *Professional Book Nerds*, https://professionalbooknerds.com
- *Library Love Fest*, https://www.librarylovefest.com
- *Worst Bestsellers*, http://www.frowl.org/worstbestsellers
- *Children's Book Podcast*, http://www.matthewcwinner.com/podcast
- *Book Club for Masochists*, https://bookclub4m.libsyn.com
- *Beyond the Stacks*, http://beyondthestacks.info
- *Cyberpunk Librarian*, https://cyberpunklibrarian.com
- *The Library Pros*, https://www.thelibrarypros.com
- *Dewey Decibel*, https://americanlibrariesmagazine.org/tag/dewey-decibel
- Public Library Association: *FYI* Podcast, http://publiclibrariesonline.org/tag/fyi-podcast

Notes

1. L. Gordon-Murnane, "Saying 'I Do' to Podcasting: Another 'Next Big Thing' for Librarians?" *Searcher: The Magazine for Database Professionals* 13, no. 6 (June 1, 2005): 44–51.
2. Steve Thomas, "Hearing Voices: Librarian-Produced Podcasts," *American Libraries Magazine*, January 4, 2016, http://americanlibrariesmagazine.org/2016/01/04/hearing-voices-librarian-produced-podcasts.
3. Brendan Dowling, "Engaging Patrons with Library Podcasts," *Public Libraries Magazine*, July/August 2017, http://publiclibrariesonline.org/2017/10/engaging-patrons-with-library-podcasts.
4. Gordon-Murnane, "Saying 'I Do' to Podcasting."
5. Rachel Evans, "Tech, Tips, and Ideas for Podcasting with or without a Studio," *Computers in Libraries* 38, no. 6 (July/August 2018): 4–7.
6. Nicole Hennig, "Podcast Literacy: Educational, Accessible, and Diverse Podcasts for Library Users," *Library Technology Reports* 53, no. 2 (February/March 2017).

Chapter 3

Flipped Learning Environments

An Introduction for Librarians Who Design and Teach

Lucy Santos Green*

Introduction

Think back to a time when you had a "peak" learning experience, a time when you learned about something or how to do something in such a way you were confident in applying that newly acquired knowledge or skills in a different context. Did you picture yourself reading an article? Listening to a lecture? Watching a show? Probably not. You may have recalled using a YouTube video to guide you through repairing a small home appliance, mastering a mathematical formula, learning to knit, having a cooking lesson with a friend or relative, participating in a team sport, riding a bicycle without training wheels, or practicing a dance for your wedding. Odds are, if you recalled an experience similar to the examples above, you described a meaningful learning event—one in which you were mentally, and often physically, engaged in activities involving gathering information, critically examining that information, and then using it to tackle a challenge or a problem.

Librarians in every setting are often called upon to engage in instructional partnerships, co-design classes or trainings, and even teach as lead instructors. Considering our backgrounds in information literacy and technology-enabled learning, librarians developing digital learning environments such as hybrid, blended, fully online, or flipped settings is a logical next step. However, before diving into flipped anything, I would like to take a moment to define and explore meaningful learning with you, the reader. I do this because first, flipping a lesson, a course, or a training flips the learning *setting* but not the learning itself. In other words, if your lesson, course, or training is poorly designed, if its design does not result in students meaningfully learning, no amount of flipping will improve it. Second, I want to define meaningful learning in this article so that you have a full picture and understanding of what I consider to be the human learning process. There are folks who disagree with me. Their definitions of learning will impact how they design and describe learning settings such as flipped classrooms. In my writings, I describe and advise the design of flipped classrooms based on the meaningful learning definition I hold dear, so that is why I would like to take a moment to discuss my interpretation with you.

Meaningful Learning

Meaningful learning is active, constructive, intentional, authentic, and cooperative:[1]

* **Dr. Lucy Santos Green** is an associate professor of Library and Information Science at the University of South Carolina. Dr. Green's research and publications center on best practices in the design of online learning environments, technology-enabled learning, and pedagogical practices for online spaces. She has authored articles and edited books on online instruction by librarians in K–12 and in higher education.

- **Active**—Students can handle objects, changing their positions and parameters, to observe how these changes affect the environments where these are located. Students can explore and experiment on their own or with others. Students have ample time to practice and manipulate information, advancing through and processing at their own pace. The activities they engage in "brew curiosity" and a desire to continue learning for enjoyment.
- **Constructive**—Students can ask questions, develop ideas and opinions, and respond, helping them build mental models to explain knowledge acquired. They connect what they are currently learning to past and future learning. With new knowledge, experience, and reflection, mental models become more involved and complex.
- **Intentional**—Students clearly understand what is expected of them and have identifiable goals in view. They are in a safe environment where they are comfortable contributing their own thoughts. Students verbalize what they have learned, reflecting on the process and the reasoning behind decisions made (they think about their thinking). They then apply the knowledge acquired to new situations or contexts.
- **Authentic**—Students complete learning activities based on real-world tasks. Learning activities based on real-world tasks are not only better understood by students, but knowledge and skills acquired in authentic contexts are also more likely to be applied to a new situation.[2] Consequently, students can demonstrate their understanding in a broader variety of ways.

The Flipped Classroom

The easiest way to define a flipped classroom is to think of it in contrast to a traditional class. In a traditional class, students are first exposed to new content through direct instruction (such as a lecture or presentation) by the teacher. For example, a student would first be introduced to the lunar cycle in a science class. In a flipped learning environment, the student is exposed to the new concept *before* the class meets. In our lunar cycle example, the student first learns about this concept by watching a video his or her teacher developed and shared, by completing a reading assignment, or by completing an interactive online activity, such as a virtual lab. Then, *during* class, students apply the key concepts or ideas they covered before class. Students collaborate with peers and the teacher *during* class through interactive and hands-on learning activities. *After* class, students use feedback gained during class activities to extend their learning by reviewing concepts they found difficult, confusing, or interesting.

Reasons for Flipping

Flipping the classroom makes it possible for teachers to reserve class time for active learning. In a flipped classroom, students wrestle with new information during class with the support of peers and the teacher. Flipping is especially popular with STEM subjects—disciplines that are traditionally difficult to tackle in depth. STEM teachers and higher education instructors credit flipping for their ability to cover a broader topic list, introduce students to complex material, and deliver hands-on, guided inquiry learning experiences during class time.[3]

Determining what a quality flipped classroom is depends upon our ability to break apart its components, anchoring each one in research-based practices. A well-designed flip reflects effective multimedia design principles, a cognitive apprenticeship approach, or an embodiment of situated learning theory. A poorly designed flip could induce cognitive overload in students, leaving them to sift through a collection of confusing or poorly supported materials and experiences without any clear connection to learning goals. Examining components for research-based practices helps us to identify good flipped classroom design choices.

For example, we know that video lectures should contain interactive components: note-taking devices, guided practice, or the ability for students to create video responses.[4] We know that students should have multiple options for sharing questions and identifying areas of struggle so the instructor can address these during class. We know that in-class activities should be student-centered, encouraging learners to meaningfully explore the content and apply their understandings to new situations.[5] Finally, any independent student learning should be scaffolded with resources available at the point of need.[6]

How Research Informs Flip Design

When reviewing research on flipped learning settings, it is possible to identify common themes in descriptions of successful flipped efforts. One might argue that solid pedagogical practice is solid pedagogical practice regardless of the learning environment and so it should not be surprising that good instructional design results in better student learning outcomes, regardless of the learning setting. As previously mentioned, *flipping* seems to integrate different pedagogical approaches. I would like to highlight a few studies that offer promising results when these are based on strong instructional design.

Talley and Scherer used distributed practice when

flipping an undergraduate psychology course.[7] Distributed practice is a learning strategy where practice is broken up into short sessions over a longer period of time. In this instance, Talley and Scherer combined distributed practice with testing and video lectures. Students viewed the lecture, then completed a practice test several times, correcting mistakes and reviewing the material. Finally, during a third session, students created their own video lecture using the information from the instructor-provided materials. In this instance, results were significant—almost a full letter grade between class sections.

Enfield combined instructional videos with note taking to flip an undergraduate cinema and television arts class.[8] He then used face-to-face class time to guide students through the application of the information presented in the instructional videos to new scenarios. While students found the videos to be helpful, engaging, and challenging, Enfield discovered that conducting in-class group activities as the only instructor was a challenge. Students had to wait for long periods of time for him to answer questions—and so in this case, flipping caused him to rethink the structure of group work in a face-to-face class.

Boucher and colleagues flipped a physical therapy course focused on musculoskeletal curricula at Texas State University.[9] As is common in the health sciences, the goal for flipping this course was to make more time for case-based learning and assessment of patient needs. By providing lectures and examples online, instructors found they could spend more time discussing content, clarifying student misunderstandings, and stressing clinical reasoning and decision-making using the Socratic teaching approach.

Several instructors required students to create and submit video responses, giving students the opportunity to explain concepts in their own words. The idea of accountability was present. Almost all studies I explored indicated the need for quizzes, short tests, or reflection posts to track student viewership of the videos created. One unexpected theme that popped up repeatedly was the need for instructors to really beef up their game in the face-to-face classroom. Freeing up all the traditional "lecture" time really placed a burden on teachers to design interactive and explorative activities. People were continually surprised at how much time and organization this took as compared to a passive lecture.

Structuring Activities Before-During-After Class

As previously discussed, flipped learning settings require that students get a first exposure to course content before class through readings or interactive videos, then spend class time deepening their understanding of that content through active learning exercises. During class, you want to limit the amount of time you lecture and increase the time students spend applying the day's material to interesting problems. Leverage the fact that everyone is in the same place at the same time by asking students to work collaboratively on problems, giving each other support and feedback. Give yourself opportunities to circulate among your students to check in on their understanding, answer their questions, and prompt them to think more deeply. Table 3.1 briefly outlines how instructional materials and activities may be organized.

"What if they don't watch/complete the activities before class?" This is a common concern expressed by librarians, teachers, and trainers who are considering flipping a course or training. When working to maintain student engagement and completion of out-of-class activities (as much as we are able) in a flipped learning environment, I find it helpful to remember that even in a traditional classroom, there will be students who choose to be absent, who choose not to complete out-of-class activities, who choose to not participate. To believe that flipping or not flipping will solve the issue of a nonactive student is to believe in a fantasy. However, I believe nonactive students, or students who do not complete out-of-class activities, do not have as much of a negative impact on flipped classrooms as might be assumed.

While unprepared students seem to defeat the purpose of flipping, this can actually result in a positive situation. Unprepared students may be paired with prepared students. This provides prepared students with the opportunity to further interact with material as they explain and review concepts with their peers, reinforcing understanding and retention in both groups of students. For those students who need even further guidance, the teacher now can dedicate time

Table 3.1. Before-During-After Class Activity Organization

Before Class	During Class	After Class
• Reading with guides • Note-taking devices • Videos • Podcasts • Web challenges • Social media • Exchanges with experts	• Teamwork • Debate • Case studies • Challenges • Hands-on projects • Experiments • Creative works • Presentations	• Social media • Self-reflection • Curation and annotation • Concepts applied to a real-world scenario • Quizzes • Comics/Stories

for one-on-one support. This would not be possible if the teacher or instructor were trying to directly teach all students at the same time.

Successful Flipping

The key to a successful flip is the key to any successful pedagogical approach—making sure that the instruction, learning activities, and assessments are properly aligned and supportive of the overall learning goals. Dr. Betina Hsieh, assistant professor of teacher education at California State University, Long Beach uses Gagné, Briggs and Wager's nine events of instruction as a helpful framework for well-aligned flipped learning settings.[10] I have summarized her thoughts below:

Event 1: Gain the Attention of Students

Consistently introduce the week's topics with a weekly email or blog post or newsletter that serves as an overview page. Introduce the topic, assignments and readings due that week, and a link to a checklist that students can use to track task completion. Dr. Hsieh recommends breaking up the checklist into pre-class, in-class, and after-class activities to facilitate student use. Short personal videos from the instructor can also be added if you are using a learning management system or a personal teaching website.

Event 2: Inform Students of the Objectives

In a flipped model, students need consistent, clear communication of the learning objectives throughout the learning process. Make sure the objectives can be located in multiple places, including the weekly overview document, the syllabus schedule of topics, the beginning of a lecture, and the beginning and end of the in-class session. This helps students to stay aware of the learning objectives in each phase of instruction while also contextualizing how goals fit together in the larger picture of the course.

Event 3: Stimulate Recall of Prior Learning

Draw on prior knowledge from previous weeks in class as well as from the lecture itself during the face-to-face sessions. However, avoid the temptation to use class time to review or redeliver a lecture.

Event 4: Present the Content

Present content outside of the course, then reinforce it in face-to-face sessions. Due dates for pre-class assessments should remain consistent throughout the semester to facilitate routine for students.

Event 5: Provide Learning Guidance

Student self-management and scaffolding are a priority. Give learning guidance in face-to-face sessions by providing opportunities for structured feedback and for lecture-based questions and discussion and by using various learning strategies. Consider scaffolding understanding of the lecture with both pre-class check-up activities and role-playing or visualizing activities in class. Remember:

- Student self-regulation and preparedness should be graded components.
- Techniques for self-regulation, study, reading response, coping with challenging readings, and interacting with group members should be intentionally addressed.
- Students should be guided through selection of technology tools for efficiency and class work.
- Check in on student comfort level throughout the flipped learning experience and adjust when necessary.

Event 6: Elicit Performance (Practice)

Make sure students participate in many practice-based activities, including scenario-based concept application and reflective writing or sharing. These opportunities for performance and practice are especially important for students as they encounter more complex challenges. When students work through these challenges, they develop deeper conceptual and practical understandings.

Event 7: Provide Feedback

Provide structured opportunities for feedback in face-to-face sessions so that students benefit from receiving consistent feedback from both the instructor and their peers. Provide formative feedback prior to assignment submission rather than solely giving evaluative feedback following submission.

Event 8: Assess Performance

The summative assessment process might remain essentially unchanged in the course flip. However, pre-class assessments should count for a small percentage of the course total points, an amount that you think is fair given that the purpose of pre-class assessments is to measure prerequisite, basic knowledge of core course objectives. The pre-assessment process is important and should not be shortchanged. It will help you assess what knowledge, skills, and dispositions your students bring to the class.

Event 9: Enhance Retention and Transfer Knowledge

The final event in Gagné and his colleagues' framework was perhaps the most important, as it involved internalization of knowledge and the ability to transfer this knowledge to a workplace setting. Make sure that your course or training flip allows for multiple exposures to concepts, as well as deeper understanding and engagement with topics for more than just the hours per week that you meet with students.

Dr. Hsieh explained: "Whether a physicist, mathematician, teacher educator or historian, we all have concepts that need deeper coverage or for which students need additional supports and regular opportunities for interaction and feedback. Through the use of consistent structures to promote learning, the flipped classroom can allow for such opportunities on a weekly basis, changing the nature and degree of teaching and learning in the classroom."[11]

Resources for Flipping

Flipped learning settings, while certainly possible without technology tools, can be designed with a broader variety of activities and assessments when technology is appropriately applied. The annotated list below includes readings and online resources that will help you consider the many options you have available when putting together your flip.

1. *The Flipped College Classroom: Conceptualized and Re-conceptualized.* Edited by Lucy Santos Green, Jennifer R. Banas, and Ross A. Perkins. Cham, Switzerland: Springer International, 2017. ISBN 978-3-319-41853-7.
    - There are several reasons why this should be your go-to manual on flipping in higher education. The book is divided into two sections. Part one includes a step-by-step guide on flipping both a shorter activity and a full course, a full chapter on tools of the trade and flipping in low-, mid-, and high-tech settings, and a thorough discussion of evaluation in flipped courses. Part two contains over thirty case studies of flipped courses in the humanities, education, engineering, STEM, and health sciences.
2. "The Flipped Classroom: Six Myths," by Kris Shaffer. Kris Shaffer website, July 9, 2015. https://pushpullfork.com/the-flipped-classroom-six-myths.
    - Kris Shaffer, PhD, is a data scientist and computational disinformation analyst for New Knowledge and Data for Democracy. With a background in digital humanities, computational musicology, and instructional technology, Dr. Shaffer addresses myths commonly held by academics regarding flipped learning settings.
3. Flipped Learning Network, https://flippedlearning.org.
    - Catering primarily to K–12 educators and K–12 teacher trainers (although in recent years a higher education constituency is now more visible), the Flipped Learning Network describes itself as "the original non-profit online community for educators utilizing or interested in learning more about the flipped classroom and flipped learning practices." Here you will find resources, professional connections, social media, a podcast, newsletter, and details about flipped learning conferences. FLN uses Slack, a team messenger tech tool that functions as Twitter should—including the option of setting up private channels.
4. Best Apps for Teaching and Learning (http://www.ala.org/aasl/standards/best/apps) and Best Websites for Teaching and Learning (http://www.ala.org/aasl/standards/best/websites).
    - The American Association of School Librarians has two committees that evaluate and select award-winning mobile apps and websites for teaching and learning. With lists going back ten years, each committee has organized award winners into searchable categories. For apps, these are Books, Content Creation, STEM, Social Sciences, Humanities & Arts, and Organization & Management; for websites, Curriculum Collaboration, Social Networking, Content Resources, Digital Storytelling, Curriculum Sharing, Media Sharing, and Manage & Organize. While the apps selected can either be free or purchased, websites selected must be free for users.

Conclusion

As you prepare to flip, do not be afraid of starting small. Take time to think through the nuts and bolts. For example, are there institutional policies that mandate what technologies you integrate in your course? Are there resources available through the university library or through a teaching and learning center? If you are hesitant about flipping solo, consider a team approach. Surrounding yourself with a supportive community will help you build on the work of others while also giving yourself the permission and room to make mistakes. When creating materials for the flipped classroom, be consistent in your design. Cover flipped classroom procedures with your students and help them to practice these procedures repeatedly. Collect feedback throughout the flip and be prepared to provide alternatives if necessary. Finally, expect that flipping a course, a module, or a training will take time. However, be assured that you are working toward the end goal—student mastery.

Notes

1. Jane L. Howland, David Jonassen, and Rose M. Marra, *Meaningful Learning with Technology*, 4th ed. (Upper Saddle River, NJ: Pearson, 2011).
2. Lucy Santos Green, Fethi A. Inan and Nancy J. Maushak, "A Case Study: The Role of Student-Generated Vidcasts in K–12 Language Learning Academic Language and Content Acquisition," *Journal of Research on Technology in Education* 46, no. 3 (2014): 297–324.
3. Nathaniel Lasry, Michael Dugdale, and Elizabeth Charles, "Just in Time to Flip Your Classroom," *Physics Teacher* 52, no. 1 (2014): 34–37.
4. Jacob Enfield, "Looking at the Impact of the Flipped Classroom Model of Instruction on Undergraduate Multimedia Students at CSUN," *TechTrends* 57, no. 6 (2013): 14–27; Lasry, Dugdale, and Charles, "Just in Time to Flip Your Classroom"; Richard Pierce and Jeremy Fox, "Vodcasts and Active-Learning Exercises in a 'Flipped Classroom' Model of a Renal Pharmacotherapy Module," *American Journal of Pharmaceutical Education* 76, no. 10 (2012): 1–5.
5. Adam Butt, "Student Views on the Use of a Flipped Classroom Approach: Evidence from Australia," *Business Education and Accreditation* 6, no. 1 (2014): 33–43.
6. Shannon Flumerfelt and Greg Green, "Using Lean in the Flipped Classroom for At Risk Students," *Journal of Educational Technology and Society* 16, no. 1 (January 2013): 356–66, https://www.jstor.org/stable/jeductechsoci.16.1.356.
7. Cheryl P. Talley and Stephen Scherer, "The Enhanced Flipped Classroom: Increasing Academic Performance in Student-Recorded Lectures and Practice Testing in a 'Flipped' STEP Course," *Journal of Negro Education* 82, no. 3 (2013): 339–47.
8. Enfield, "Looking at the Impact."
9. Brenda Boucher, Eric Robertson, Rob Wainner, and Barbara Sanders, "'Flipping' Texas State University's Physical Therapist Musculoskeletal Curriculum: Implementation of a Hybrid Learning Model," *Journal of Physical Therapy Education* 27, no. 3 (2013): 72–77.
10. Robert M. Gagné, Leslie J. Briggs, and Walter W. Wager, *Principles of Instructional Design,* 4th ed. (Fort Worth, TX: Harcourt Brace Jovanovich, 1992).
11. Betina Hsieh, "Step by Step, Slowly I Flip," in *The Flipped College Classroom: Conceptualized and Re-conceptualized*, ed. Lucy Santos Green, Jennifer R. Banas, and Ross A. Perkins (Cham, Switzerland: Springer International, 2017), 33.

Chapter 4

Taking Your Library Instruction to YouTube

Heather Moorefield-Lang

When the discussion began for this issue of *Library Technology Reports*, I knew I wanted to focus on different types of technologies and digital resources for library information and instruction. As the editor for this report, I sought librarians who blogged and created podcasts. I looked at colleagues who created virtual and augmented reality tours and instructional models. I had a range of peers who taught online and used a host of digital resources and applications in their face-to-face as well as online instruction. I have served on or have been chair of the American Association of School Librarians Best Websites for Teaching and Learning Committee since 2008. I knew how to talk about technology with instruction. These experiences are what led me to the creation of my own technology channels based on YouTube. For my chapter, I wanted to delve into the journey of my two YouTube channels. This issue of *Library Technology Reports* originally came from a discussion about these channels and why they had been created in the first place. This chapter dives into why I chose to create instructional video channels, how I created my own channels, the topics I picked for my focus, and recommendations for practitioners, as well as resources for your own channels.

Why I Chose to Make Videos

I have been delivering professional development face-to-face or at a distance for almost twenty years. In my early years as a librarian, I would train my peer educators on HTML, videography, Dreamweaver, Microsoft Word, PowerPoint skills, and a variety of district-based technology. As the years passed, the training became more complex. With the introduction of Web 2.0 tools and interactive digital resources, I started delivering workshops on best websites, digital storytelling tools, online presentation resources, citation sites, databases, and much more. When tablets and handheld devices arrived on the scene, I started delivering training on topics like best apps, storage of tablets for libraries, application mashups, and technology integration. The years continued, and the websites, applications, and technology continued to change with the times. There will always be new resources, technologies, and tools to demonstrate, share, and teach.

In 2014, I received a full-time teaching position as an assistant professor at the University of South Carolina. During my interview, I discussed my professional development workshops with the faculty of the School of Library and Information Science. They seemed to be excited to have someone interview with them who had professional training and technology experience. Their concern revolved around timing. What happened if someone couldn't come to a training? What would I do if faculty members or peers in other departments wanted to attend a workshop and missed the opportunity? My response during my interview at the time: video.

Before I joined the faculty at the University of South Carolina, I was working as an academic librarian at Virginia Tech. In that job, I typically would teach live or synchronously in face-to-face as well as online formats. I was also commonly creating short videos using Jing to answer reference questions for my faculty and students. These short videos had offered a new option for short reference and instructional interaction. Creating videos for professional development seemed to be a logical and simple step.

Once I started full-time at the University of South Carolina, I began my first channel. I called it *Tech Fifteen*. Originally, I wanted to call it *Tech Five*, as in take five or a short break, but that name was already taken. This was my introduction to branding. The focus of the site was to have short five-minute videos that focused on a specific online tool or resource. The format was simple: introduce the tool or resource, feature the highlights, and discuss how it could be used with instruction. The content was easy; there were always new technology tools, websites, applications, and resources being released. I would find the ones that best applied to the field of librarianship and education and feature those on my site. All technology tools shown on *Tech Fifteen* were free or free at some level (some had a subscription level for more memory or space). I decided to create a website to further brand and extend the reach of the YouTube videos. I also share each video on Twitter as it is made. All videos are closed captioned and Creative Commons–licensed for accessibility and embedding.

In 2017, we had a statewide conference with a focus on information literacy skills in the K–12 schools of South Carolina. The School of Library and Information Science at the University of South Carolina decided to further work with this statewide initiative. It was during this time that I created my second YouTube channel, *Research Xpress*, a channel where young people, middle-to-high-school-age students, could seek aid in their information seeking and literacy skills. This was also a channel for librarians and their peer educators, a place to aid them in the explanation of concepts such as keywords, databases, presentation skills, and citations.

There have been successes and challenges with each channel. Currently, in 2019, both channels are still up and running. As the person creating and editing the videos, along with producing the channels alone, I can say there is a consistency issue with releasing videos. My original plan was a new video each week. That idea fell through quickly. Currently, I am pleased with one or two videos a month. Audience was an issue, especially with my second channel. Creating a channel for peers in the field of librarianship was easy; creating a channel for teens was a challenge. I have many questions for myself on content, video length, and usefulness. Sustainability is a common concern as well. When you are solo in the creation of a product, it will be difficult to sustain it forever. In truth, these projects were never meant to have a permanent or enduring shelf life. They are created and often archived to meet a need at a particular time. My fellow authors would possibly say the same thing about their blogs, podcasts, vlogs, and more. They are wonderful while they last but can't remain forever.

Creating Videos

There are a variety of items to consider when creating a good instructional or informational video. The following is a selection of topics on which to ponder.

Audience—Who is the intended audience of your videos or video channel? For *Tech Fifteen*, my audience includes librarians, peer educators, and anyone else who might like to learn about different types of technology tools, online resources, and digital apps. From my YouTube analytics, my videos have been viewed by teachers, librarians, university students, and professionals in business and industry—all adults. For *Research Xpress*, the channel was intended for middle-to-high-school students as well as young people looking for research skills at the early secondary education level. I know that educators and librarians have also used these videos in their instruction. It is important to have an audience in mind when you are creating your material. This also will aid you in your tone, content, and length of video.

Length—Keep your videos short, especially if you are delivering an instructional video. No one wants to watch a thirty-minute video. Personally, I am keen on five minutes. They are easy to view and absorb, and if my audience likes what they see, they can always watch more. My videos are asynchronous, not offered in real or live time. This is the not the same as creating a class, course, webinar, or online workshop. Those will typically be longer, will commonly be offered live (synchronously), as well as recorded for archival purposes and future viewing.

Content—What type of information or instruction do you plan to impart? If you have decided to start your own YouTube channel or video series, then you must have something to share. Is there something you are passionate about in your field? Have you noticed a topic missing from conversations, blogs, social media feeds, and more in librarianship, technology, archives, or reference? Do you have a friend with whom you love to converse, and you feel everyone would benefit from those professional conversations? Do you have an amazing space, ideas, lessons, instruction, or plans that you want to share with world? This is how you narrow a focus for content.

Technology—If you look at the resources listed below, you will find many useful online resources for video creation and storage. Other types of technology to aid in the success of making a video can include a webcam and a microphone. A webcam that includes a microphone can really take care of everything. You really don't need a headset microphone. Talk clearly and loudly, using the microphone in the webcam, and you will have a nice sound.[1] I personally have a webcam and a separate mic. I am a fan of the Blue Nessie microphone—it isn't super expensive, and the sound quality can't be beat for the cost.

Accessibility

When talking about accessibility and videos, you are mainly looking at captioning and narration. If you are not interested in captioning, make sure to provide transcriptions of your videos. If you are on top of your game as a professional or instructor, you provide both. There are a variety of tools and services to aid in video captioning. YouTube (see Tools for Video Creation) will caption videos for you, but editing the captions is typically required. Rev and other transcription services are excellent resources to know when looking to have videos transcribed for your viewing audience. Transcribing isn't too difficult if the video is short. If the video is longer, then the transcription obviously takes more time. If you have the funds to pay for transcriptions, I highly recommend doing so.

Narration in a video is very important. If you are offering professional development, instruction, and information, it is important for your viewing audience to know what is occurring. Explain what is on the screen, spell out links, and guide your users through the instruction. Make sure they understand what is happening visually and through your narrative.

A final note on accessibility is a look at file types. How you format your video and the types of files that you use for your videos matter. Currently, HTML 5 is a good format for video viewing and playing. YouTube creators can choose to have videos played in the HTML 5 version. Depending on the type of video production tool you use (Camtasia, Screencast-O-Matic), you can choose to save your video in HTML 5. Why is this important? Accessibility across devices. There is a great deal of flexibility in being able to view a video on a laptop, handheld device, or phone. It's a wonderful option to provide your viewers the chance to watch videos at home or in line getting a cup of coffee. Accessibility across devices is highly useful for your audience.[2]

Resources for Video Creation

The following is a selection of tools to help in the creation of your own videos.

Screencast-O-Matic: https://screencast-o-matic.com. When you need to create how-to or flipped lesson videos for your library or classroom, then Screencast-O-Matic is a great option. Simply choose online what you plan to record or narrate over a set of slides. This online tool is incredibly easy to use and free for up to fifteen minutes of recording time. It is a great instructional tool for teacher librarians and peer educators but also appropriate for K–12 students.

Camtasia: https://www.techsmith.com/video-editor.html. If you are familiar with Jing, then you know the company that created Camtasia, Techsmith. Camtasia is a screen recording, video creation tool that performs similarly to Jing and Screencast-O-Matic. The main difference is that this is a subscription-based product, and there is no limit to your video length. Camtasia also offers a variety of options like captioning, zooming, panning, fades, and more.

YouTube: https://www.youtube.com. You may use YouTube for your educational or entertainment video needs. YouTube can also be a wonderful curation location for all your videos. Once you have created a video, simply load it into YouTube, label and choose settings, and you are ready to share. YouTube also has automatic captioning for accessibility purposes, which you can easily edit. YouTube provides a useful platform for instructional and informational videos.

Vimeo: https://vimeo.com. Another popular video platform, Vimeo is a location to house your video creations. It is not free, but you won't have to deal with ads, and for some creators, there is comfort in that. Vimeo's community is not as large as YouTube's, but you have a more concentrated, supportive group of viewers. When it comes to accessibility, the video creator has to provide the transcripts and captions. When deciding where you want your videos housed, audience is important. For whom are you creating these videos? Where would you like them to live once they are created?[3]

Kapwing: https://www.kapwing.com. Kapwing provides a multi-tool solution for teachers, librarians, and students to create everything from video montages and memes to stop-action videos and sound effects. It is a very valuable tool for video editing as well. Its simple yet robust platform makes it useful for students of all ages. If you are looking for a user-friendly editing tool that offers a wide range of options, Kapwing is worth taking a look.

Rev: https://www.rev.com. If you are looking for a transcription company, Rev is a great option. It is one name among many in the transcription business, but it is my personal favorite. Why might you need a transcription service? For videos, captioning or transcriptions are very important for accessibility. Typically, you can choose one or the other. Both is the best. For my podcasting friends, transcriptions are very important in making their audio files fully accessible. Rev not only provides transcriptions, it also translates your subtitles into other languages and provide captions. It is not free, but it is very reasonable for a transcription service.

Blue Microphones: https://www.bluedesigns.com. Blue Designs offers a wide range of microphones and headsets for computer and music recording as well as gaming. There is also a selection of recording tools to sync with your handheld devices for interviews. Microphones are available across a wide range of prices, and most are very reasonable.

Sample Online Video Resources

Look at the following online video sources for good educational content or as examples for your own online video. There are many YouTube channels and other online video sources in the field of education and technology—the list below is just a tiny, selected sample.

Tech Fifteen: https://www.youtube.com/TechFifteen. My YouTube channel that I created in fall 2014. This channel is focused on technology integration. Each video focuses on one technology or digital tool or application. I show what the tool is, show how it can be used, and share ideas for instruction for librarians and peer educators.

Research Xpress: https://www.youtube.com/researchxpress. My second YouTube channel created in spring 2017. After seeking ideas to further aid middle- and high-school students in their information-seeking and literacy skills, I started this channel to aid librarians and their fellow teachers. This channel takes the viewer through different information-seeking skills such as finding keywords, using different databases, presenting information, and creating citations.

Physics Girl: https://www.youtube.com/physicsgirl. A resource for physics videos and other science material. Dianna Cowern, the creator, has a Twitter feed and website with all sorts of physics goodness. This is a channel that makes science fun and exciting.

Free Technology for Teachers: https://www.freetech4teachers.com. Richard Byrne has created a blog about resources that educators and librarians can use in their learning spaces. In his blog, he has videos in many of his entries to further explain the technology he is discussing.

TED-Ed: https://ed.ted.com. TED-Ed is all videos for education. Launched in 2012, this video database has something for everyone. There are videos, animated videos, lesson plans, a global network of educators, and much more. TED-Ed brings a myriad of educational videos to your laptop, tablet, or phone.

Vlogbrothers: https://www.youtube.com/vlogbrothers. Created by John and Hank Green, *Vlogbrothers* is a video blog (vlog). The two brothers have celebrated over ten years on YouTube. Followers of their vlog are called Nerdfighters, and the topics of their YouTube series are wide and varied. A wonderful example of a show that celebrates education, science, and the nerd community.

Notes

1. Michael Smedshammer, "10 Tips for Creating Effective Instructional Videos," Faculty Focus website, Magna Publications, March 31, 2017, https://www.facultyfocus.com/articles/teaching-with-technology-articles/10-tips-creating-effective-instructional-videos.
2. University of Minnesota Disability Resource Center, "Accessible U: Video Formats," accessed March 19, 2019, https://accessibility.umn.edu/multimedia/video-formats.
3. Justin Simon, "YouTube vs. Vimeo: What's the Difference?" *TechSmith Blog*, May 15, 2018, https://www.techsmith.com/blog/youtube-vs-vimeo-whats-the-difference.

Chapter 5

A Librarian's Journey in Blogging

Lucas Maxwell*

Blogging can be a useful educational tool with numerous benefits for both the student and the educator. It allows for reflection, the cataloging of important data and events, and sharing information with others. A professional blog can also be used as a way to track and monitor educator and librarian professional development and act as a résumé. For students, research shows that blogging improves writing and self-confidence and connects them to other educators and students around the world.[1] I hope this chapter will inspire librarians and their peer educators to begin a professional blog as well as encourage their students to begin the process of blogging.

I started blogging in 2013 when I began my new position as school librarian at Glenthorne High School in south London, UK. I created a site using Blogger for the Glenthorne High School Library. The school did not have a qualified librarian before I started the post, and considering I hadn't worked in a school library before, I wanted to catalog my adventures in this new world. The problem was that I didn't really know how to blog effectively. I hadn't really written a blog or post before, and to be completely honest, I was intimidated by the whole process.

Glenthorne High School Library
https://glenthornelrc.blogspot.com

Blogging became a necessity when my manager asked for monthly reports on what was happening in the library. She was hoping for basic statistics, which I was, at the time, delivering in an email. I then provided monthly borrowing statistics along with which books were most popular with the students. We also had a library count gate that told us how many students were visiting daily. I was able to tally these numbers up every month and send them to my administrator. All these statistics gave her the numbers, but not the story of what was happening in my library.

After a few failed attempts at creating a newsletter for the library, I finally landed on using Blogger as a primary form of communication with my manager and, eventually, the outside world. I chose Blogger as my format because I found it easy to use and share with others. I always included a lot of photos in my blog posts, and Blogger lets you add these and other features, such as outside links and clean templates, easily.

The blog quickly evolved into more than just statistics, though. In addition to providing basic monthly stats, I started capturing both the challenges and positive events that took place in the library. Blogging soon became the perfect way to tell my manager and other members of the senior leadership team at the school what I was doing in the library, what I was aiming to do in the future, and how I hoped to achieve these goals.

It was also an amazing way to connect with teachers and other staff at the school. Starting out in a large school can be intimidating, and librarians are typically an isolated group in the school. Creating a blog and highlighting all the cool, interesting things we were doing while also showcasing student work and events made the blog an extremely valuable tool. I would send the blog link out to teachers every three months as a reminder, and the response was always very positive.

Sending a link to my blog to parents via email and promoting it during events such as prospective

* **Lucas Maxwell** has been working with teens in libraries for close to ten years. Originally from Nova Scotia, Canada, he spent five years as a teen services librarian. He then moved to the UK and became a high school librarian at Glenthorne High School in South London. In 2017 the School Library Association named him the UK's School Librarian of the Year. He lives in southeast England and writes for the website Book Riot and *School Library Journal* in his spare time.

parents evening and parent council were also effective ways to introduce myself to them and the students alike. I asked our IT team to integrate the blog into the school's virtual learning environment (VLE). Now, when students log in to the VLE to download and complete their homework, they can also click on the library blog button and see what's been going on and what events are upcoming.

I'm happy to see that Blogger is still listed by many sites, such as TechRadar and ThemeIsle, as one of the top blogging platforms to use. Blogger allows users to customize their blog to a certain extent by choosing from a variety of themes and customizing the main header. I did this by branding the blog with the name of the library and including an attractive photo of the library below. It's simple and to the point.

This doesn't mean that Blogger is the only route to take. There are plenty of user-friendly, attractive-looking platforms out there that you might find easier to use. One of the most popular blogging platforms is WordPress, which "now 'powers' over a fifth of the internet."[2] WordPress is very easy to use and extremely popular with bloggers and with companies hoping to create an identifiable brand.

There's also Tumblr, Live Journal, Medium, Squarespace, and countless others. I suggest taking a few for a test drive and finding what works best for you.

I also use Weebly for a YA book review blog; it's very easy to use, and users can customize it with images and different styles to fit their needs. I personally wouldn't use Weebly for more in-depth discussion, as I do on Blogger, but for adding a flashy image of a book and writing three or four paragraphs about it, it's perfect. Like Blogger, Weebly also allows users to integrate ads and have a Twitter feed running live along the side if that's something of interest. Weebly's interface is primarily drag and drop, which makes it perfect for people like me who can sometimes be intimidated by new technology.

Benefits of Blogging

There are many benefits to blogging, both professional and personal. On a professional basis, it allows you to create and manage your identity. My blog is now the hub for everything I do professionally. Every post I create is tagged with labels, a practice I highly recommend if you are starting your own blog. It's very helpful when it comes to searching for relevant blog posts you have written in the past. For example, if I want to find out what professional development courses I took or conferences I spoke at over the course of a year, I simply access my blog and click on the "professional development" tag that I created for each post reflecting on these events. The search results will display every blog post with that tag, and I can easily access the information I need.

Tagging can also be valuable for reporting. Since I have tagged all of my blog posts that contain borrowing stats with related labels, if my manager or another member of the senior leadership team at school asks for any stats, I can have them ready in a matter of seconds. Collecting statistics from the first month of my first post in 2013 was a great decision as it has allowed me to see how far the library has progressed and where we need to go in the future.

I regularly use tabs on my blog to help other librarians or educators to access information that I think could be beneficial. Within these tabs, I have collated all my information literacy and library lesson plans, links to my YA book review site, the monthly library newsletter that I publish, and more.

Tabs are also useful to keep information literacy tips at the ready. I created a series of infographics highlighting ways to avoid plagiarism, note-taking skills, copyright information, and website evaluation a few years ago. I include them in the tabs to ensure that other educators can access them quickly and provide feedback if need be.

I also created several reading lists that are easily accessible via my blog. Reading lists are often requested by our English team to use in their classroom, and I try hard to keep them up-to-date and relevant. Having them on my blog means that teachers can access them at their convenience and provide me with quick feedback if they think anything needs to be altered or updated.

Using a blog, I have my entire professional career at my fingertips. Having a blog with your name on it will also send people in the right direction if they search for you. This will help other professionals learn about your work and hopefully share your good practices.

Blogging will teach you many things. On the face of it, you will learn basic technical skills that are required to publish your work online. By blogging and sharing your work, you will also connect yourself to other bloggers in your field. By reading, sharing, and understanding other people's perspectives, you'll become much more informed and involved in your library and education community.

Through blogging, I haven't simply added new followers to my social media channels. I have developed true friendships and positive professional relationships that have made me a better librarian. If you stick with blogging long enough, you will develop a devoted group of followers for idea exchange. One of the most surreal and exciting moments for an introverted librarian blogger such as myself is attending a conference and having other librarians approach me to say they really enjoyed reading my blog. It's a feeling that never gets old and is an amazing way to develop connections that will benefit everyone.

I know for a fact that becoming a blogger and sharing the blog through social media has resulted in being asked to speak at library conferences and events. If you are consistent, positive, yet honest, you will develop a following that will want to hear what you have to say. Speaking at events and conferences will connect you to experts from around the world and help highlight the great work you do to even more like-minded professionals.

Your blog can act as your résumé in many respects. It is a professional portfolio that you can showcase if you find yourself seeking employment in a new location or sector. Using it as a base for everything you do professionally will only create positive outcomes.

Reasons Students Should Blog

There are several benefits to having your students blog. Whether this is in the classroom or library on a regular basis, it doesn't really matter. Blogging will exercise the creative muscle that can be softened with more formal approaches to education. Blogging allows students a huge amount of creative freedom that can be used to develop their own voice and perspective, which will become essential when they enter the workforce. It also allows them to respond to constructive criticism, and if allowed to develop their own theme and style, they will learn new technical skills.

I've already touched upon the importance of regular writing when it comes to improving our professional work. We know this works for adults who are full-time authors. Imagine how effective it would be for students who start to write and blog regularly at a young age. It will help teach them routine and the importance of committing to a project. It also develops that professional portfolio I mentioned earlier, something that, if they stick with it, they can refer back to and reflect on at an early age. At Glenthorne High School, I ask students in years 7 and 8 (grades 6 and 7) to blog their book reviews, which I then convert into a magazine shared as a PDF document.

Student blogging isn't just about them speaking their minds, it's about improving their self-confidence. Writing is known to help young people become self-aware and to aid in the understanding of personal experiences, writes educator Kathleen Morris.[3] Having students write regularly about their work, successes, failures, and challenges will help improve not only their self-worth but also their communication skills.

Having students blog and comment on each other's posts on a regular basis, when monitored by a teacher, will improve spelling and grammar, to name just one benefit. Kathleen Morris, who has her students blog daily, says that her students' literacy and engagement levels dramatically increased.[4] Reluctant writers wrote with a purpose in mind, and students used their blogs to communicate with each other.

Parents can also access and view their children's blogs, which creates an instant connection with what's happening in the library or classroom to the family at home. Encourage parents to get their children to blog at home to keep the writing and reflecting activities happening.

Blogging is an opportunity to teach students about creating a positive digital footprint. I feel that we engage in a lot of scare tactics when it comes to teaching students about being online and their digital footprint. There are reasons to be ultra-cautious; however, it's also important to ensure students are engaging positively in the online world because blogging is a way for them to start their digital footprint in a controlled, positive way.

Getting students engaged in blogging also allows them to see things from other people's perspectives. If you have students reflecting on a lesson, news, or a social topic, they will see that not everyone shares the same opinion and how important it is to be considerate of others' views. This can help generate civilized debate and discussion to carry forward on a daily basis.

Blogging can be used to connect students to other classrooms around the world. Having different classes comment on other students' posts is the perfect way to electronically introduce them to new places and cultures. Our students' adventures in blogging have led to Mystery Skypes and several other collaborations with other groups of students around the world. Mystery Skypes are a fantastic way for students to learn and create global partnerships. Students Skype with another group, and the classes are unaware of each other's geographic location. Using a series of yes-or-no questions and using atlases and iPads with Google Earth, students must try to pinpoint the other class's location.

We have read the same book together and discussed it on Padlet; we have shared recommended reads via Flipgrid. We've gone low-tech and shared postcards with each other, recommending books and discussing our favorite first lines of literature. Blogging has been the launchpad for all these activities and many more.

Promotion

I promote my blog in different ways. The primary way is social media such as Twitter and Instagram, with Twitter being the preferred format for me. I created a link to my blog on my Twitter profile to ensure it's the first point of contact people see when they access my Twitter profile. I also always have a pinned tweet that will lead them to a certain event I'm promoting through the blog.

To properly publicize it, I post at least once a week, sometimes more than that if I feel the need. At the end of each month I do another post to showcase the highlights and the most popular books. To showcase the top ten books of the month, I do a running countdown on Twitter on or near the last day of every month. Each tweet counts down the top ten books, tagging the author and publisher if applicable, and including a link to the blog. This is a great way to bring new people to the blog and promote what I do.

I send a reminder link for the blog out to teachers every few months. I do this routinely no matter what's going on, but I also send it out in between those times if we have a special event approaching. For example, we ran a weeklong series of events in the library under the theme "Harry Potter vs. Hunger Games," where students competed in various literary events to see which series was more popular. To promote this event, I made an animated video using an online video program, Powtoon. I then embedded the video into my blog and sent a link out to all homeroom teachers in the school.

Activities like these bring positive attention to a blog and allow the user to create a wider audience. Having the blog link on an email signature, creating bookmarks with the blog address and other social media handles printed on them, and making postcards that highlight the library's services that can be placed in staff pigeonholes are ways that I've promoted the blog within the school.

What to Blog About?

When I first started blogging, I didn't really know what to write. I felt self-conscious mainly because I thought I was doing nothing but patting myself on the back. This feeling soon dissipated, however, after I realized that nobody was going to do this for me. In addition, librarians (especially in the UK) are having to prove their worth more and more as budgets are slashed dramatically. There's absolutely nothing wrong with patting ourselves on the back and sharing it with the world.

I started blogging about author visits, clubs I had started, student artwork, and library stats. It evolved into a lot more than that, though. I started reflecting on challenges I've faced, how I've approached behavior issues in the library, how I've struggled with the negative perception of comics and graphic novels, and a lot more. These are the posts that have generated the biggest responses, and I have really benefited from sharing these experiences with the larger education community.

I also collect data from previous posts and write another post serving as a guide on that topic. For example, I found that I had been posting weekly on what our manga/anime club had been doing—what successes and challenges I had with it, and even blogging about my complete failures when they happened. This resulted in a post that served as a guide on starting your own manga/anime club, where the pitfalls were, how to draw people in, how to keep them there, and what manga to purchase for your high school library. Sharing this post led to several other librarians to share their own stories about starting their own manga/anime clubs, and we were able to spread that information in various social media formats to others who may have been considering starting their own.

My advice would be to simply start writing. Show off some of your favorite library programs—tell people what worked, what didn't, and what you'd do differently in the future. Share a basic craft program, for instance Zines, in detail because what might seem second nature to you might be completely new to someone else. I am inspired and incorporate other librarians' ideas often (always giving them credit, of course), and 99 percent of the time I will find that great idea on someone's blog.

Blogging has, without a doubt, changed my career for the better. It has connected me to my profession in a way I never expected; it has led to several new professional opportunities; it has established my place in the school that I work; and it has allowed me to reflect on my professional life in a thoughtful and effective way. My hope is that others will enjoy the same experience if they are inspired to start their own blog after reading this.

Notes

1. Kathleen Morris, "Why Teachers and Students Should Blog: 18 Benefits of Educational Blogging," Kathleen Morris website, March 14, 2018, http://www.kathleenamorris.com/2018/03/14/benefits-blogging.
2. Diana Soare, "18 Best Blogging Platforms of 2018," Drsoft.com, December 12, 2017, https://drsoft.com/2017/12/12/18-best-blogging-platforms-of-2018.
3. Morris, "Why Teachers and Students Should Blog."
4. Morris, "Why Teachers and Students Should Blog."

Chapter 6

Final Thoughts

Heather Moorefield-Lang

In this issue of *Library Technology Reports*, we have discussed podcasting, creating YouTube channels, flipped learning, and blogging—all valuable tools that you can consider implementing to elevate your instruction. The authors have featured a variety of ways to get started, gather ideas, and execute and use these technologies in delivering instruction and information. They have discussed challenges with the technologies, offered recommendations, examined obstacles faced, and shared success stories. Through digital media, these authors have been able to deliver a wide range of information to a vast group of people.

My final thoughts to you are these. What are you interested in sharing? We all have information to impart because we all have individual and independently lived experiences. Your peers, colleagues, and fellow professionals want to know what you know.

As you consider exploring a new technology to enhance your instruction, think about the following:

1. What you do every day in your practice. Is there something that you do well, something that you specialize in? Would you be willing to share your expertise? There are a variety of ways to do this.
2. Where you work. Are you in a rural (urban, suburban, international) library setting? The field wants to hear about experiences that are different from theirs. They are also very interested in hearing about situations like their own. Which leads me to the next point.
3. It is so easy for us to become professionally lonely in this field. School librarians are typically one to a school. Public librarians can be siloed in their setting depending on the location. Academic librarians are commonly very specific to their field. Those are only a few examples. No matter our location, community, or setting, we are going as fast as we can. We crave information from the field, and when knowledge is shared among peers, it is amazing.
4. The tools that are available to you. If you're not interested in blogging, vlogging (video blogging), podcasting, and so on, know that there are other tools out there. Start small—create a newsletter for your school, system, district, or community. There are a variety of digital newsletter tools available (Smore, Canva). There are a variety of template-based, easy-to-use website tools available where you can build your own webpage for information and instruction distribution.
5. If sharing information or teaching using technology makes you extremely nervous, watching what is available. The authors of this report have recommended a host of podcasts for listening, YouTube channels to view, and blogs to read. Take a look, see what is out there, absorb, learn, and if you decide you would like to join these authors in information sharing, know that the option is always available.

Notes

Notes

Library Technology REPORTS

Upcoming Issues	
August/ September 55:6	**Planning and Implementing a Sustainable Digital Preservation Program** by Erin Baucom
October 55:7	**Privacy and Security Issues for Library Systems, 2019 Edition** by Marshall Breeding
November/ December 55:8	**Blockchain in Libraries** by Michael Meth